Unattended

Alan Catlin

Cyberwit.net
HIG 45 Kaushambi Kunj, Kalindipuram
Allahabad - 211011 (U.P.) India
http://www.cyberwit.net
Tel: +(91) 9415091004
E-mail: info@cyberwit.net

Printed at Repro India Limited.

"I've
plagiarized my life
to give you the best
of me."

Ocean Vuong, *Time Is a Mother*

"In the sentence, "She's no longer suffering," to what,
to whom does "she refer"? What does the present
tense mean?"

Roland Barthes, *The Mourning Diary*

"This ain't no disco,
This ain't no fooling around."

Talking Heads

Contents

1-Prologue

Veronica Lake: Martha Washington Hotel, 1962

I wonder how many
patrons (men) remarked
that the new bar maid
seemed familiar. There
was something about
the look: her hair, the way
she moved. Wondered
how many companions saw
the look in their men's eyes
How they thought: what's
familiar about her is that
she's a woman, a bit down
on her luck but once upon
a time might have been a beauty.
How often the women said,
"Aren't I enough for you?"
The women saw the hard
miles on the bar maid,
and the men saw the blonde
hair, thought how she might
have looked, once upon
a time.

Roni, Martha Washington Hotel, 1962

She wished her man
would just drop the subject.
Give him a couple of blasts
and every woman turns into
a sex object, a movie
star down on her luck.
It was obvious what
the new girl had going
for her: man trouble, tons
of that. Too much to drink,
not enough sleep. A couple
of years and she'll be lucky
to walk a straight line.
He said, "No, seriously.
Subtract ten, maybe fifteen
years, drop a few pounds,
put her in nice clothes with
better foundation garments,
and you've got something
special there."
She thought: Everybody was
somebody once when they
were twenty-five. It's been
a long time since she was
anything like twenty-five.
Said, "More than few pounds
and clothes won't help her now."
"I'll bet her name is, Roni.
Go ahead, ask her."

"You ask her and while you're
at it, order me another
Manhattan. I'm going to
the little girl's room."
He raises his arm to attract
the girl's attention. She knows
he won't ask her anything.
He's such a coward. Decides
to end this discussion here
and now. Says, "She calls
herself Connie."
"How do you know that?"
"It says so on her name tag."
Leaves the last part of what
she was thinking, moron, unsaid.
Connie, Martha Washington Hotel, 1962

Connie de Toth was
her working name then.
Interviewed by reporters
later on, she said, "I took
the job because I like
people. I like to talk to
them."

The hell she did.

Connie Talking

Cocktail waitressing
wasn't the same as
talking to Alan Ladd
in *This Gun for Hire*

The Glass Key
The Blue Dahlia

In another life

Martha Washington Hotel, 1903

was exclusive, women
only, even then. Was
the first of its kind in
New York.

Even the employees:
desk clerks, hostesses,
chaperones, elevator
attendants, cleaning
staff, lounge workers,

all of them women.

MWH, 1902

450 Rooms. En suite
included. Catering to
traveling women on
business or holiday.
A rarity then.

What kind of woman
travels on business
or goes on a holiday alone?

MWH, 1902

The location was (is)
prime centrally located
near surface and subway
transport. Reasonable rates:
$1.50 a day and up
with a restaurant on
the ground floor for men
and women, a telephone
in every room.

Contemporary Post Card of MWH, 1902

shows the lobby
listing all pertinent
details and rates

29 East 29th Street

80 years later the lobby
looks the same though
much shabbier

Looks like furniture
might have been
replaced

The rugs.

Looks like something
Edward Hopper might
have painted with a
hangover

After a fight with
his wife.

Louise Brooks

resided at the hotel
she called, "A respectable
women's hotel downtown."

Probably thought it
was an acceptable
alternative after
a humiliating eviction
(for unknown reasons)
from the Algonquin.

Brooks also wrote,
"The atmosphere
of the Martha Washington
was institutional. The women
wore short hair, stylish
and sensible shoes, and
worked, I presume, in offices."

Said she was, "assigned a
cell under the roof."

Was asked to vacate
the premises, "because
people in a building
overlooking the hotel
were shocked to see
me exercising in flimsy
pajamas."

One wonders what
those flimsy garments
were?"

What did they expect
a woman to wear while
exercising? A union suit?

Veronica Lake, 1960's

Despite a series of now
classic movies in a noir
mode, Veronica had serious
issues. Her co-star
in *Sullivan's Travels,*
Joel McCrea refused to
act with her again.
Said, "Life's too short
for two films with
Veronica Lake."

Screenwriter/novelist
Raymond Chandler called
her Moronica.

She developed a reputation
of being difficult to work
with. Marilyn Monroe
could get away with being
a diva but Veronica?
She was just Connie
from Florida and Marilyn
was always Marilyn.

What that translated
in everyday language
was, "She was a bitch."

If you were a man
it meant you were an
asshole.

She began arriving on set
drunk or hungover unable
to remember her lines.

When berated by directors
or fellow actors for
her faults, she walked off
set in a huff.

Her earnings peaked at
forty-five hundred a week
in the 50's. Sick money.
She could work a hundred
years as a cocktail waitress
and be lucky to make
that much in tips in a year.

Still, she was no Barbara
Peyton reduced from being
married to star Franchot Tone,
making the same kind
of money in the 40's
and living in a mansion to
a five dollar a pop whore living
in a junkie hotel with
champagne tastes but drinking
rot gut wine instead.
That was Peyton in her 30's.
Her movies occasionally turn

up on TCM, Veronica's
at film festivals.
Acute insults to the liver
didn't care about pedigree.
Cirrhosis claimed her at 54.
Payton didn't make it nearly
as long.

2-Unattended

The Body According to Detective Evans

The cleaner found
her face down on
the floor. A little
blood, no marks
indicating assault.
Natural death: only
your coroner knows
for sure.

Detective Evans Room #641 MWH

Looks like just
another: one minute
you're with us,
the next minute
you're not, stiff.
Pretty simple,
really. No warning,
no pain, just bingo,
you're gone.
We should all be
so lucky.

Room #641 MWH

Large open floor plan.
No en suite. Outlets
for small "college room"
fridge, hot plate, sink
for washing up, small
counter space, five drawer
dresser all contents
dumped on unmade queen
size bed, large walk-in
closet, contents dumped
on floor. Now a repository
for random junk/
possessions. Sealed for ten
summer weeks with DO NOT
CROSS police tape.

No fire escape, window
hermetically sealed.
80 years of NYC soot
and grime on each panel
smeared as if someone had
tried to clean a space to
look out. And failed.

Surrogate Court Offices, NYC, circa 1985

Not quite *Little Dorrit*
Department of
Circumlocution though
In-use-ledgers look
like something Dickens
would be familiar with:
four feet high and two feet
wide, at least, hand written
pages containing vital records,
must weigh a hundred
pounds. Printed pamphlets
outline office procedures.
All must be followed to gain
access after all-important
Tax Waivers are secured
from pre- 9-11WTC tax office.
Not one computerized record
anywhere. Assertion that
Surrogate Court is last in
priority line for modern
record keeping, duly noted.

Housekeeping

Sometimes we find
them. The ones who
have passed on. She
was not my first and
probably not my last.
Some of the girls
don't call it in right
away. They search for
cash and jewels. Take
their wedding rings,
if they have one,
just like hospital
staff. Not me. I call
downstairs. Say
a little prayer. It's
the least I can do.

NYC Coroner's Office

All the unattended ones
must be autopsied. It's
the law. Half of them
were never going to be
claimed anyway so it's
not like we should be in
a hurry to cut them open.
It's not like they're going
anywhere. Anywhere other
than Hart Island.

Some are easier than others.
The last one came down
from Martha Washington
was a Y incision and a couple
of peeks inside. No doubt what
she died of. Big time cancer
everywhere. Sew that one up
and make it go away. Even
the paper work was easy.

Her cousin saw

her in the City
a week before she died.
"You'd never know
she was that close
to passing on. Of course,
she was thin but
then she always was.
Seemed happy and
talked like there
was no tomorrow.
How did she die?"
I told him that
when they opened
her up, after finding
the stomach cancer, they
didn't look any further.
Was enough cancer there
to kill two people.
"Stomach cancer.
That's supposed to be
painful, isn't it?
She showed absolutely
no signs of pain.
We went McDonald's
and she ate like a horse."
"I expect her dissociative
personality gave the pain
to someone else. I asked him,
"What did you do when

she started talking crazy?
How did you handle it?"
"I just laughed and
laughed and eventually
the subject changed."
He was the kind of
guy to just deal with stuff,
make the best of things.

He identified the body too.

Detective Evans

People automatically
assume that when you are
told to investigate an
unattended death that
there's a crime involved.
Like murder. Not so.
Mostly what you have
to do is a boring routine.
What you have is your
standard room or rooms,
when it's outside, you
might be surprised how
many unattendeds there
are outside dumped in
alleys, under park benches,
in the bushes. Those can be
pretty hairy. Anyway, like
this one at Martha's you
have a room and a closet full
of personal crap you have
to sort through looking
for valuables. By valuables,
we mean cash, jewelry, stock
certificates, obvious stuff
that might be worth something.
Generally speaking, we turn in
most of the stuff we find.
We can flexible about some
prescription drugs and private

stashes. Stuff is only going to
get chucked anyway, so what
the hell? Cash too. Ten per
cent per guy, per case, is
the going rate. Some guys want
to take it all but that wouldn't
be right.

Neighbors

You'd think they'd never
seen or heard of someone
dying in their room the way
they stare and whisper to
each other. It's undignified.
You have to feel bad when
someone goes, alone, without
friends, lovers, maybe even
family. It's not like Beverly
had visitors or anyone saw
her out with anyone. Mostly,
kept to herself by choice.
You have to respect that.
That's why they call them
private rooms. She wasn't
one for small talk, that's for sure.
And that year of hopping…
I asked her what was the matter
with her foot and she said,
"Nothing. It's good exercise."
I was going to ask her why it was
all swollen and discolored
but the look she gave me…

Well, it said leave me alone.
So, I did.

Mr. Santos, Hotel Manager

As long as the weekly
rates are paid we will
respect the tenant's privacy
and leave her belongings
intact and in place.
Not all hotels do this.
Beverly was with us
for many years and never
missed a payment.
Although she is no longer
with us in body, she is
with us in spirit and her
account is current we will
maintain the space until
her legal situation is resolved.
It is unfortunate that the ending
of our long relationship
should be terminated this way
but deaths do occur in resident
hotels like ours. We expect
to meet with her representatives
in the near future.
We did take the liberty of
removing all perishables from
#641. Sometimes these things
take time to be resolved.

3-Before

Housekeeping

Beverly was a strange one
Who knows how she ended
up this way. I mean, you can
tell she had some nice things
before she let herself go.
Clothes that cost real money:
coats, shoes, all way out of style
but still…. Not that you ever saw
her in anything but cast-offs
that street people wear.
She wasn't no street person,
though. Paid regular in cash.
Not that there was ever much
she would let me do in #641.
Very fussy. Don't touch this,
don't touch that. God only
knows what was in those paper
bags she had everywhere
on the counters…

And dark. I never see a room
as dark as the way she kept that one.
Black curtains on top of curtains.
like a tomb. Creepy. And that
little altar…. I don't like to think
about that. All those burnt-down-
to-different-heights colored candles…
Yes, she was a strange one.
I do what she say, nothing

more, nothing less and we get
along just fine. It's a job. Do what
you are told and don't ask questions.
Works for everyone in the end.

Lunch Counter

Who are we today, Bev?
The good girl, right?
Otherwise, it's out we go.
You know how it works and
you damn well know I mean
what I say. No messing around,
I am not in the mood. No one
is in the mood today. Am I
getting through to you?
Acting out is for little kids.
And talking dirty is out,
period. Way out. You know
what I mean? Like, you fuck
with me and I'll fuck with you.
Pretty simple, right? Good.
Now that we understand
each other, Hello, how are you?
What can I do for you today?

Corner Store

It takes all kinds.
I try to remember my lessons
as a child, "We're all God's
children." We need to be patient
and tolerant and respectful but
after years of people stealing,
some kids as young as six
lifting things right in front
of you, bold as you please,
and their momma's talking back
when you accuse them.
Threatening you. And then their
big brothers breaking windows.
It's like they expect you to let
them take stuff. Like it should
be free. Like I don't have to
pay for the stuff they steal out
of my hard-earned money:
twelve hours a day, six days
a week, all my life.
And now, holdups with guns.
I blame the drugs. They are not
in their right minds. Who is these
days? So, a crazy lady who buys
the same thing every day,
same time, seems like a small
drop in a big leaky bucket.
Kool filters. Two soft packs.
Four on Saturday. She breaks

off the filters. Lights up.
Maybe she feeds the filters
to the birds or the fish in
the ponds? What do I care?

OTB

Man, that Beverly chick is
one far out bitch. Every day,
a full card, two-dollar windows
only. Studies them forms like
they be religious books.
Making her notes in the margins.
I wonder what the hell she
writes? What the hell she's
thinking? No doubt she has
a system. The whack jobs all
have system's but none of them
are retiring rich. You'd think
that after a while, with all that
losing that they would understand
that their sacred systems don't work.
No. They think the system just
needs a minor adjustment and
then…Then, nothing. But she
seems to win. Sometimes anyway.
I guess I'm her lucky window.
What's she going to do when
I'm gone?

Neighbors

The Martha Washington used
to be a respected place for
single ladies to rent by the week.
I'm not saying that it has lost
all of its allure, it hasn't, but
people like Beverly, well they
bring the rest of us down.
Maybe not to her level but
there is a guilt by association.
She doesn't fit in with respectful
ladies. It's her manner, the way
she dresses like she just got out
of a poor house or a mental
institution. You see these people
everywhere these days. Mostly in
the subways and on the street,
in the parks. The state just up and let
them go, no how do you do,
just see you later, don't call us,
we'll call you never. But you don't
see them in nice hotels. Or you
shouldn't. What's the world coming to?

On the Street

She be one fucked up lady.
Yeah, man. What you think
she hopping around for?

She got fire in her ass or
something?

Maybe we could go ask her?

Fuck that. We might get
what she has.

You think it's contagious?

Hell yeah, gotta be.

Soon everybody's gonna be doing it.
A street full of hopping
loonies.

I can see it, man.

Yeah, me too.
Think we should take her?

Fuck no, man, she ain't got
nothing we need.

Corner Newsstand

I got 'em ready before I see
her 'cause I know she be by
any minute. Easier just to give
her the forms, take the money
and now how ya do. Know what
I mean? The Daily is her standard
Usually, it's the old guys know
those things backwards and
forwards: pedigree, track conditions,
win loss records, fast tracks,
slow tracks, mudders, shit, she
can give you chapter and verse.
Seen it myself. Heard it myself.
Never seen a guy try to take
her down twice. Make a fool out
of a professional handicapper.
Maybe she's one of those
crazy millionaires you read
about. She owns a stable
and gets her kicks fucking people's
brains up. Bet she wins too.
One thing for sure she keeps coming
back regular as clockwork.
Gotta have some money to do
that. Someday a chauffeur gonna
come and pick her up. Take her
to the flat track in style.

In the Subway

That there's Bud the CHUD.
He's a wild one alright.
You think it was bad down
here before, the last few years
it's been hell on wheels.
I mean whole armies of people
coming down here make the guys
you see in the stations and on
the streets talking to themselves
and stinkin up a storm, seem
downright normal. They got whole
abandoned stations and tunnels
occupied, man. Like they're fixin'
to invade. Bud, he's like a scout,
near as I can figure. Checking out
the opposition topside and checkin'
their resources. We'd better be
ready 'cause when they start
to move, there's going to be serious
issues. I mean like big time trouble.
CHUD's man are another thing starts
with a C serious as cancer.
What's a CHUD? You serious?
Cannibalistic Humanoid Underground Dwellers.
Didn't you see the documentary?
That was no made-up thing, that was
Real life shit. I seen 'em down there.
Don't take my word for it, check it
out for yourself: the 91st street station
is home base. The 18th is a forward base.
People like that woman you talkin' about
thrive on this shit.

The Phone Call

Is this the K- residence?

Yes. May I ask who is calling?

This is Detective Evans from Midtown South Manhattan precinct.

What's she done now? Is she in trouble again?

I can't explain over the phone. Someone from your local precinct will come to your home shortly and explain what happened.

We don't have precincts up here.

Someone from your local department will explain to you.

She's not in trouble then, is she?

No, far from it.

I get it.

4-Aftermath

After the phone call

We wait.

For the rookie to try and explain the worst possible news someone can get.

The young cop is clearly more upset than I am.

Red faced and stammering.

I save him from trying to find the right words he cannot possibly have.

She's dead, isn't she?"

Yes, she is.

I want to buy him a drink.

He clearly needs it more than I do.

5-Talking Heads

Midtown South Manhattan

"The busiest precinct in
the world," says a plaque
over the doors that usher
you inside the station.

What does it look like?

Ever see a police drama
set in NYC?

That's what it looks like
because all the sets are
modeled after a station
just like this one.

At least, that's what it looked
like in 1985.

Probably hasn't changed much.

Except now their records
are, maybe, computerized.

One Police Plaza

If you look up Brutalist
Architecture in a Pictionary
the illustration would show
this office building conceived in
a nightmare by Franz K and
executed by someone who
adhered to the code that:
all memories of degenerate
(classical) art must be destroyed.

"In the basement we hear the sound
of machines," sang David Byrne
and the Talking Heads.

He must have been down there,
in the Property Shack where
the deceased one's "valuables"
are stored.

Behind a cage stands the clerk
from the story by Franz K.,
"Before the Law," who you would
have met, if somehow, you
managed to get inside the castle
and tried to move farther into
the bureaucratic maze.

This clerk has the ultimate power
to deny you the property

that is rightfully yours,
and will, if he possibly can.

All you have to do is
prove who you are and all issues
will be resolved.

Simple, right?

Inside One Police Plaza
Wrong.

One Police Plaza

Without a drivers' license.
A passport
A valid NYC library card
(Out of town doesn't count)
A birth certificate copy
A Duplicate Draft Card
Who am I?

Difficult to determine.

Maybe impossible.

Midtown South Manhattan: Detective Evans

You can tell a boat load
about a person by
what he or she leaves
behind.

Some collect stuff
You know like stamps
Post cards
Coins
Crap Jewelry
Shitty art
Dolls
Whatever

Racing forms, though,
that was a new one
You could tell without
looking too hard she took
that shit serious

Annotations in pen
and pencil and magic markers

Drawings and arrows
Underlining
Cross referencing
What the fuck?

Then I thought

Not my problem

Midtown South Manhattan: Evans

I guess the bottom line
about the MTW stiff
was she was one
strange cat

I mean we found a denim bag
full of stock certificates
she must have dragged
with her through
the depths of the city
given the ragged look
of it

Takes all kinds
I guess

The altar threw me, though
She burned stuff in a little
dish

All kinds of colored candles
One for every day of
the week, I guess

Weird

Not my problem

If you think about
this too much it
fucks with your head

It just isn't worth it

Besides they'll be another
stiff tomorrow

Or later today

Life sucks
then you die

You know what I mean?

One Police Plaza Property Shack

Seven pages of property
vouchers, precisely numbered
and indexed, one certificate
per line

Dozens of lines

Painstakingly checked
and slid across the counter
from the cage to the airless
place where I am waiting

wondering
not for the first time:

what the fuck is this?

What does it all mean?

One Police Plaza

Hours of this

Entered a nightmare
as a pauper and
emerged as someone
else

Someone who needs
a broker

There is no comfort
in this

On the subway

Leaving Chambers Street
heading uptown for
Midtown Manhattan

A battered briefcase
full of documents
inscribed with imaginary
numbers

Confusion and dread

Despair is a hotel room

But I don't know
that yet

Midtown South Manhattan

The Tuesday after Labor
Day 1985. The cop who
gives out the "jobs"
isn't interested in assigning
a detail to open a sealed room
in the MWH. There are so
many more important jobs:
a mugging in the park
an attempted robbery on 34th
armed robbers at Chase Manhattan
a body on

Midtown South Manhattan

You might as well be
invisible to the desk sergeant

He shuffles you upstairs
to the detectives

They send you back downstairs

You need a uniform

They're all busy

New ones are reporting
for shifts every ten minutes

Are sworn in right there
by the front desk

You watch them enter as civilians
and transform themselves
into heavily armed warriors
but none of them

are available

for you

Midtown South Manhattan

The plain clothes
dick says to me
"The room will be a bit
of a mess."

My look says,
"What the fuck?"
He says, "I recognize
the handwriting on
the paperwork. It's mine."

He doesn't say,
"Have a nice day."

He knows better than that.

No one ever has a nice day
in Midtown South Manhattan.

Detective Evans

I almost feel bad for the kid.
He looks so lost and
clueless. He'll learn
quick.

Hey, they pay us to look for
stuff, not be neat about it
or clean up after.

It might not be the worst
day of his life
in that room
but it will rate
right up there
with the worst.

Midtown South Manhattan

One thing I know about
cops is they hate being
stared at. And they know
when someone is doing it.

It's the kind of feeling
that gets under your
skin and makes you
out of sorts, then it makes
you nervous, and eventually,
it drives you crazy.

I figured he was good for
a few minutes before it
got under is skin then
he will be compelled to make
the feeling go away…

Make me go away.

So, I stare just to let
him know: I am never ever
going away ever. Not until
you delegate unforms to
take me across town
to the hotel and open
that fucking seal.

In a cop car driving cross town

Listening to the calls.

To the cop talk

About their crazy friend
who emptied his weapon
again.

He oughta know by now
they count those shells
and they need to know
where they went.

He knows.

So, what's his problem?

He likes shooting at people.

You mean he's hunting niggers again?

You said it, not me.

You going to the game this weekend?

You bet.

Bringing the wife?

Yeah, got to.

Your girlfriend won't like it.

Very funny.

She'll be there.

Yeah, yeah, give me a break, will ya.

Best drunk of the year.

Yeah, after last year I hope you saved
up a lot of sick time.

Hey, what's an intra-departmental softball
game without a fist fight.

A softball game. You don't have
To punch people.

You don't?

Never mind…

It's a slow day after the holiday
weekend. Only one attempted
rape, an assault, one armed,
and a purse snatching in ten
minutes driving cross town.

6- Room #641

Inside

After the removal of
the yellow crime tape

the unlocking of
fading red painted
fire door

the stepping inside
is no simple
entering

into a once living
person's room
but a transformation.

Finally, Inside #641

Is what Jack
Nicholson sees
in *The Shining*
when he steps inside
Room #217
of the Overlook
Hotel

Inside #217/#641

The ghosts
are alive

have seized
control of
the narrative

Once Inside

Inside #641
you can sense
the body

feel its presence

feel the restless
spirits clamoring
for release

Inside

The overwhelming
smell of confinement
three months

of closed-in
for a summer
stuff

soot and ash
and smoke
and dust;

dead stuff

Inside

"A bit of a mess,"
the cop said.

Looks like they
searched the room
with a wrecking
bar

Pillaging, is more
like it

Ransacking

Plundering

Ravaging

Looking for
valuables.

Whatever their
definition of
valuable was

Certainly isn't
clear to me

is why we are
the inexactness of

the definition
of words

like valuable

The rest is
rubbish

Inside

I guess saving account
bank books don't
count as valuables

Inside

Check books
either

Inside

Motherfuckers

Inside

Personal Identification
documents:

Birth certificate

Driver's License
(expired)

Notary Public Stamp
(expired)

Library cards:

New York City
(active)

Overdue NYC library
book notices
(Active: Dante's *Inferno*
Goethe's *Faust-Part 1*)

East Rockaway Public Library
(expired)

Certificate of Residency/
Work Permit Virgin Islands
officially stamped St Croix 1953

Divorce Decree

Social Security Cards
under three names

some variations on the theme
of Beverly K.

Inside

Motherfucker

Inside

A room filled
with junk

So much shit
to wade through

Where to begin?
Where to end?

The smell

The lack of air

The dead stuff
all around

overwhelms

Inside

It appears as if
everything
that entered
this room

no matter how
useless

remained

Inside

After an hour
of sifting through
the wreckage of
a human life
becomes more
like soul searching
than a legal
necessity

All the legal and
financial stuff

All the odd lots that
fit inside
a suitcase

are packed

Art Books:

Blake
El Greco
Bosch

Some poetry,
of all things,

books

variations on a theme
of heaven and hell

Inside

The diaries
in the form
of letters
outlines
a way of life

the philosophy
of the separation
of the mind
and body

into component parts
on alternate
worlds

where the body
does not
die

Inside

Letters
that refer
to the holy
codex
as outlined
on the daily
racing forms

lost now

forever

incinerated now
like the body
that lived
here

7-Coda

Housekeeping

Once the responsible
party has left
Beverly's room,
the girls want to
help me with the mess.
I tell them I need
some time alone.
I think of these
women as my ladies,
my sisters, in a way,
and our agreement
is: I will not invade
their private world,
as these rooms
are their homes
and I am employed
to keep their space
as neat and as clean
and as private as I can.
The girls don't respect
that. They feel that
they have no lives of
their own, why should
they care about someone
else's? They don't pay
us enough for us to care.